Sean McCollum

Lerner Publications Company • Minneapolis

Lerner Publications Company
A division of Lerner Publishing Group, Inc.
241 First Avenue North
Minneapolis, MN 55401 U.S.A.

Website address: www.lernerbooks.com

Library of Congress Cataloging-in-Publication Data

McCollum, Sean.
    Kenya / by Sean McCollum.
        p. cm. — (Country explorers)
    Includes index.
    ISBN 978–0–8225–8661–6 (lib. bdg. : alk. paper)
    1. Kenya—Juvenile literature. I. Title.
DT433.522.M38 2008
967.62—dc22   2007024891

Manufactured in the United States of America
1 2 3 4 5 6 – PA – 13 12 11 10 09 08

Table of Contents

Welcome!

Let's explore Kenya! Kenya sits on the continent of Africa. To find it, just look for Africa's biggest lake. That body of water is called Lake Victoria. It touches Kenya's southwestern edge.

The Indian Ocean touches Kenya too. It laps the nation's southeastern shores. And plenty of land surrounds Kenya. Sudan, Ethiopia, Somalia, Tanzania, and Uganda are all Kenya's neighbors.

MILES

0		50		100		150		200

0	50	100	150	200	250	300

KILOMETERS

Lake Victoria is so big that it's in three countries! It stretches into Kenya, Tanzania, and Uganda.

4

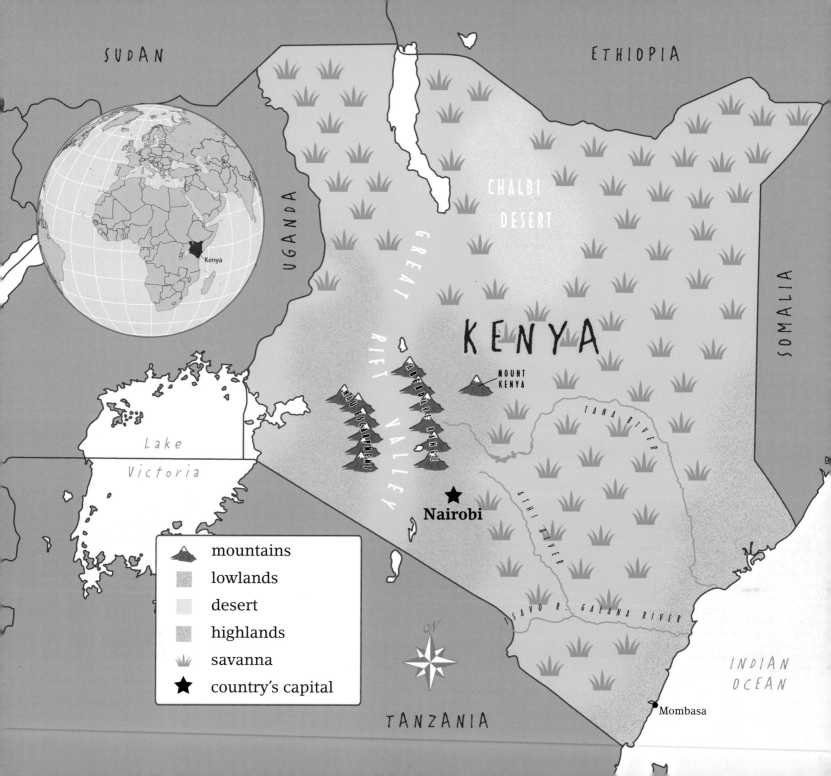

SUDAN

ETHIOPIA

Kenya

UGANDA

GREAT RIFT VALLEY

CHALBI DESERT

KENYA

SOMALIA

MAU ESCARPMENT

ABERDARE RANGE

MOUNT KENYA

TANA RIVER

Lake Victoria

ATHI RIVER

Nairobi

TSAVO R. GALANA RIVER

mountains
lowlands
desert
highlands
savanna
country's capital

N

TANZANIA

INDIAN OCEAN

Mombasa

Highs and Lows

Southwestern Kenya has mountain ranges. This part of Kenya is called the highlands. The highlands get cool weather. Southeastern Kenya is covered with sandy coasts. This part of Kenya is known as the lowlands. The lowlands get very hot.

White sand covers this coast in Kenya's lowlands.

The highlands and the lowlands both get a lot of rain. Many people live in these two regions. Most Kenyans are farmers. They need the rain to help their crops grow. Between the highlands and the lowlands lies the savanna. The savanna is a grassland. It is dry. Few Kenyans live there.

Trees called acacias dot Kenya's savanna.

Land of Animals

Grab your camera! We're going on a safari. A safari is an exciting journey. It's a chance to explore a country's landscape.

Travelers drive over the bumpy savanna to see Kenya's land and animals up close.

On safari in Kenya, you might spot lions, elephants, and giraffes. You may see a rhinoceros lumbering through the grass. Kenya is also home to many birds. Pelicans, storks, and pink flamingos live near Kenya's waters.

Tall giraffes tower over Kenya's grasslands.

Early Peoples

Many different ethnic groups live in Kenya. The people of an ethnic group share a religion, a history, and a language.

These children are from an ethnic group called the Samburu.

Kenyan languages are much like languages spoken in other parts of Africa. That's because Africans from the west, north, and northeast moved to Kenya long ago. They pushed out or joined the people who were already living there.

Kenya's different ethnic groups have their own languages and traditions.

Many Peoples

Most Kenyans' ancestors came from other parts of Africa. Ancestors are relatives who lived long ago.

Most people in Kenya are native Africans—like this smiling group of children. Native Africans' ancestors are from Africa.

Some Kenyans' ancestors came from other continents. Arabs and Europeans both settled in Kenya. In 1895, Britain took control of East Africa. During British rule, Indians came to help lay railroad tracks in Kenya. Many Indians stayed in the country.

A small number of Indian families still live in Kenya.

Who Are You?

The way Kenyans live depends a lot on whether their ancestors settled in the highlands, lowlands, or savanna. In some villages, the people are expert farmers or fishers. Talented craftspeople live in other places.

A skilled Kenyan carpenter displays a carved chair.

In parts of Kenya, groups of herders travel from place to place. They move in search of food and water for their animals. Traders and businesspeople often live in the cities.

Pulling Together

Kenyan leaders want citizens to practice *harambee*. This word means "pull together" in Swahili. Swahili is a Kenyan language. Pulling together is a tradition in Kenya. People work with one another to grow crops and raise their families. But pulling together isn't always easy. The people of Kenya come from many different backgrounds. Sometimes it's hard for Kenyans with different histories to pull together.

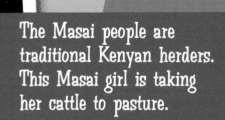

The Masai people are traditional Kenyan herders. This Masai girl is taking her cattle to pasture.

Big City

Nairobi is the capital of Kenya. It is the nation's largest city. People from all over the country come to live or to sell their goods in Nairobi.

Tall skyscrapers line Nairobi's bustling streets.

Nairobi is a busy place. For fun, you can visit the city's restaurants and movie theaters. You also can see wild animals! Nairobi National Park is home to ostriches, giraffes, and buffalo.

Visitors to Nairobi will find plenty to do.

On the Move

Few Kenyans own cars. Most people take buses and trains to get from place to place. They also ride in vans called *matatus*.

Trains are one way to get from place to place in Kenya.

Matatu drivers take Kenyans wherever they want to go. Many riders squeeze into one matatu. If you ride on a matatu, be sure to hang on tight! Drivers travel quickly over Kenya's bumpy roads.

Brightly painted matatus speed along Kenya's streets.

Village Life

Do you know anyone who lives on a farm? Many Kenyans live in farming villages. Village kids have busy days. They help their moms raise food, cook meals, and wash clothes.

A Kenyan girl pedals a water pump on her family's farm. The pump brings water to the crops.

Kids with younger brothers and sisters often babysit for them. And some Kenyan children also go to school. But when chores are done, village kids make time to play.

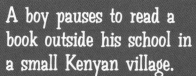

A boy pauses to read a book outside his school in a small Kenyan village.

Family

Most Kenyan kids have big families. Grandparents, aunts, and uncles are important family members. Kids sometimes stay with them while their parents go to work in the city.

Masai family members pose for the camera.

Family Words

Here are the Swahili words for family members.

grandfather	babu	(BAH-boo)
grandmother	nyanya	(NYAH-nyah)
father	baba	(BAH-bah)
mother	mama	(MAH-mah)
uncle	mjomba	(mm-JOHM-bah)
aunt	mbiomba	(mm-bee-OHM-bah)
son	bin	(BEEN)
daughter	binti	(BEEN-tee)
brother	ndugu	(nn-DOO-goo)
sister	dada	(DAH-dah)

Kenyan families are very close. Relatives often live near one another. They stick together and help one another.

Family life is important to Kenyans.

23

Home Sweet Home

Some Kenyans live in modern houses or apartments. These homes have plumbing and electricity.

Both modern high-rises and older buildings with iron roofs stand in Mombasa, Kenya.

24

Other Kenyans live in simple homes. Houses in the village might be made from wood, grass, and mud. To make a snug roof, Kenyans might weave palm leaves together.

Do Not Waste a Drop!

If a village does not have running water, kids and their moms must carry heavy containers full of water from wells—sometimes for several miles. Other families can afford to pay someone to deliver jugs of water.

Homes are made of wood in this poor Kenyan neighborhood.

Shared Language

Each ethnic group in Kenya has its own language. But lots of Kenyans also speak Swahili. Kenyans use Swahili when they meet in the market or at work. That way, they can understand one another.

The people of Kenya speak many different languages—but when they get together, they might use Swahili.

English is another common language in Kenya. It is the language of government and international business. Kids study English in school.

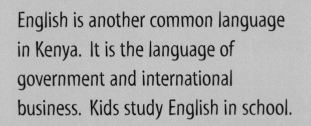

What language do you think these Kenyan children speak?

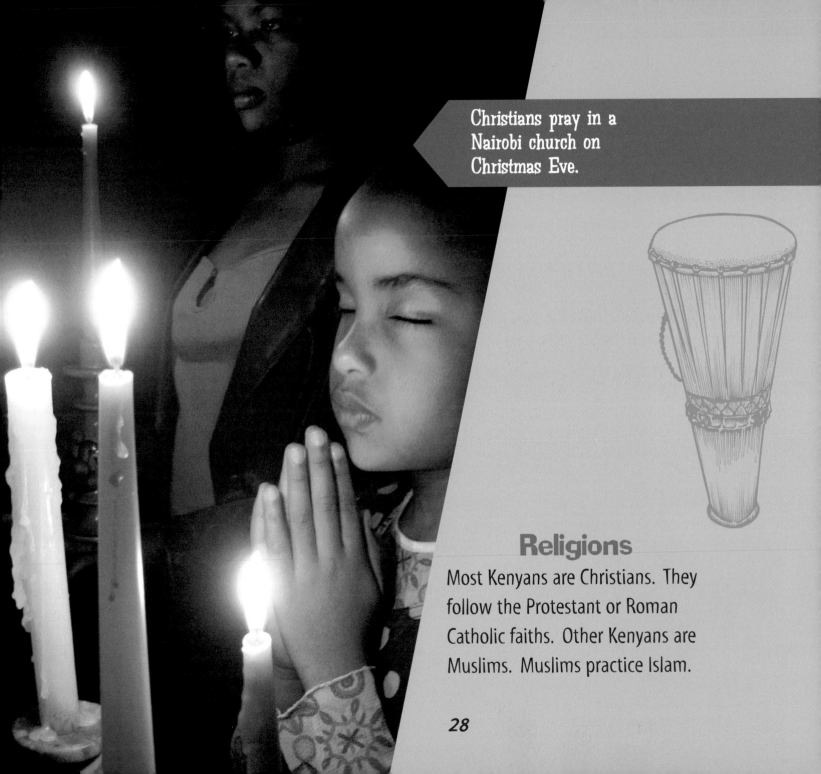

Christians pray in a
Nairobi church on
Christmas Eve.

Religions

Most Kenyans are Christians. They
follow the Protestant or Roman
Catholic faiths. Other Kenyans are
Muslims. Muslims practice Islam.

28

Some Kenyans follow ancient African religions. These religions teach that spirits live in rocks, trees, and animals. Many ethnic groups mix African faiths with Christianity.

Mombasa

Dear Grandma and Grandpa,
Hello from Mombasa! That's the city where we're staying. Mombasa is an island. Dad says it's also a port. That means huge ships can drop off and pick up goods. Lots of people in Mombasa are Muslims. Muslim women wear outfits called *buibuis*—long black dresses and head coverings. And guess what else? The roofs of mosques—the buildings where Muslims worship—look just like onions!

See you soon!

Grandma a
Your
Anywh

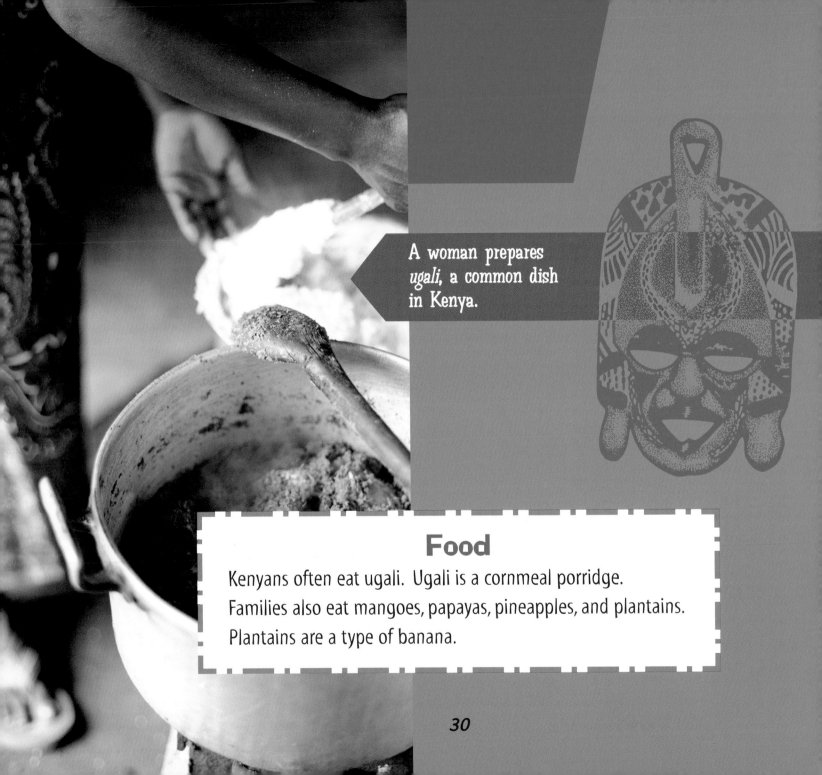

A woman prepares *ugali*, a common dish in Kenya.

Food

Kenyans often eat ugali. Ugali is a cornmeal porridge.
Families also eat mangoes, papayas, pineapples, and plantains.
Plantains are a type of banana.

30

Kenyans who live near water eat fish. Goat and beef are other popular meats. For a snack, Kenyans enjoy roasted corn.

Bananas are among the items for sale at this Nairobi market stall.

School Time

Kenyan students study subjects such as Swahili, math, and geography. Children must wear uniforms in school.

A group of elementary school students lines up to have their picture taken.

Elementary school is free for Kenyan students. But not all children are able to attend. Some stay home to help their families instead.

A Kenyan student reads in class.

These Kenyans are celebrating Kenya's Independence Day.

Celebrate!

Kenya became a free country on December 12, 1963. Each year, city dwellers celebrate with big parades. Musicians and dancers wear fancy costumes. Many people return to their home villages to spend the day with relatives.

Religious holidays are important to Kenyans. Christmas and Easter mean the most to Christians. Ramadan is sacred for Muslims. Ramadan is the Muslim holy month. Muslims fast from dawn to sunset during Ramadan. That means they do not eat during that time.

Kenya's Muslims raise their hands in prayer during the month of Ramadan.

Sports and Games

On your mark. Get set. Go! Kenya's runners are fast. Their talents make them world famous. But Kenyans also enjoy team sports. Their favorite is soccer.

These Kenyan runners won gold, silver, and bronze medals at the 2007 World Championships in Athletics in Osaka, Japan.

Safari Rally

Each year, an amazing car race comes to Kenya. It's called the East African Safari Rally. In this race, drivers speed across roads in Kenya, Uganda, and Tanzania. Racing fans should not get too close to the roadside—cars sometimes spin out of control.

When Kenyan kids aren't kicking a soccer ball, they try to beat one another at checkers. They also like a board game called *kigogo*.

Many kids in Kenya enjoy playing soccer. What do you like to do for fun?

Dance and Music

Kenyans perform dances for births, weddings, and funerals. These dances are a tradition in Kenya. Traditional songs go along with the dances.

Samburu dancers demonstrate a traditional dance.

Modern music is popular in Kenya. *Benga* is a kind of dance music. Benga combines guitar sounds with bass rhythms.

A Kenyan man plays a stringed instrument.

A man sells colorful Masai craft items.

Everyday Art

Kenyans like to make everyday objects beautiful. Some folks dye fabrics. Others create jewelry from colorful beads or metal.

Carving is an age-old Kenyan skill. Craftspeople make drums, masks, and stools from wood. Kenyans also carve animals out of soapstone. Soapstone is a soft rock.

These beautifully carved statues come from Nairobi.

Story Time

Kenyans love good stories. Animal tales are popular. Storytellers create a special voice for each creature.

A mother reads a story to her son.

Be sure to find a cozy place to sit! A good storyteller can go on for hours.

Sneaky Rabbit

Have you ever heard of Bre'r Rabbit? This critter is a character in African stories. He always wins because he plays tricks on stronger animals. Bre'r Rabbit is a smart but sneaky creature. In one Kenyan language, the word for rabbit means "the one that sleeps while his eyes are open."

Kenya has a high literacy rate. This means that most Kenyans can read. These Kenyan sixth graders are reading a newspaper in their school's library.

THE FLAG OF KENYA

Kenya's flag has black, red, and green bars. White stripes run between the bars. The black bar stands for the people of Kenya. The red bar stands for the struggle for freedom. The green bar stands for Kenya's natural resources. The white stripes represent unity and peace. A shield and spears sit in the middle of the flag. These stand for Kenya's pride, tradition, and the defense of freedom.

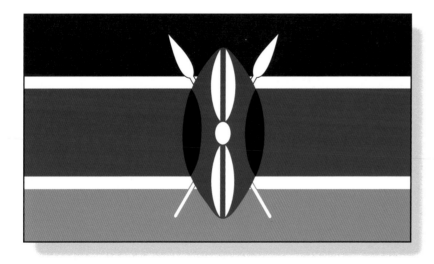

FAST FACTS

FULL COUNTRY NAME: Republic of Kenya

AREA: 224,960 square miles (582,644 square kilometers), or slightly smaller than the state of Texas

MAIN LANDFORMS: the mountain ranges Aberdare Range and the Mau Escarpment, the volcano Mount Kenya, the Great Rift Valley, the Chalbi Desert

MAJOR RIVERS: Athi, Galana, Tana, Tsavo

ANIMALS AND THEIR HABITATS: lions (high plains), buffalo (high plains), elephants (high plains), rhinoceroses (high plains), leopards (high plains), pelicans (coast), storks (coast), flamingos (coast)

CAPITAL CITY: Nairobi

OFFICIAL LANGUAGES: English and Swahili

POPULATION: about 36,913,721

GLOSSARY

ancestor: a relative who lived long ago

capital: a city where the government is located

continent: any one of seven large areas of land. The continents are Africa, Antarctica, Asia, Australia, Europe, North America, and South America.

ethnic group: a large community of people that shares the same religion, history, and language

highland: an area with hills or mountains

lowland: an area that is lower than the surrounding land

map: a drawing or chart of all or part of Earth or the sky

mountain range: a group of mountains. Mountains are parts of Earth's surface that rise high into the sky.

religion: a system of belief and worship

safari: a journey, often in Africa

savanna: a tropical grassland

TO LEARN MORE

BOOKS

Chamberlin, Mary. *Mama Panya's Pancakes: A Village Tale from Kenya.* Cambridge, MA: Barefoot Books, 2005. Adika invites all his friends to eat his mother's pancakes—but will there be enough for everyone? Read this Kenyan tale to find out.

Haskins, Jim, and Kathleen Benson. *Count Your Way through Kenya.* Minneapolis: Millbrook Press, 2007. In this picture book, you'll learn more about what makes Kenya special—from unique arts and crafts to amazing wild animals.

Lynch, Emma. *We're from Kenya.* Chicago: Heinemann, 2006. Meet Kenyan children and read all about their country's landscape, culture, and geography.

WEBSITES

Africa for Kids
http://pbskids.org/africa/
Listen to a Swahili folktale, make fun African masks, and learn more about the continent of Africa on this website from PBS.

Kenya
https://www.cia.gov/library/publications/the-world-factbook/geos/ke.html
This site features many useful facts about Kenya.

INDEX

The photographs in this book are used with the permission of: © Images of Africa Photobank/Alamy, pp. 4, 24, 34; © Jon Arnold Images/SuperStock, p. 6; © Adam Jones/Visuals Unlimited, p. 7; © age fotostock/SuperStock, pp. 8, 16, 17, 29; © Michele Burgess/SuperStock, pp. 9, 27, 32; © Michael Lewis/National Geographic/Getty Images, p. 10; © Sue Cunningham Photographic/Alamy, p. 11; © Sean Sprague/Peter Arnold, Inc., p. 12; © Trip/Alamy, p. 13; © Zute Lightfoot/Alamy, pp. 14, 19; © Neil Cooper/Panos Pictures, p. 15; AP Photo/Sayyid Azim, pp. 18, 28, 31, 35, 43; AP Photo/Tom Maliti, p. 20; © Nick Cobbing/Alamy, p. 21; © Nicholas Pitt/Alamy, p. 22; © Sven Torfinn/Panos Pictures, pp. 23, 25, 26, 37 (top); © James Baigrie/The Image Bank/Getty Images, p. 30; © Betty Press/Panos Pictures, pp. 33, 42; AP Photo/Itsuo Inouye, p. 36; Simon Maina/AFP/Getty Images, p. 37 (bottom); © Jim Tampin/Alamy, p. 38; © Eric Wheater/Lonely Planet Images, p. 39; © Wolfgang Kaehler/Alamy, p. 40; AP Photo/Hal Smith, p. 41.

Illustrations by © Bill Hauser/Independent Picture Service.
Cover: © Thomas Cockrem/Alamy.